2024

THIS IS THE YEAR FOR:

THIS BUJO OF SHADOWS BELONGS TO:

THIS BUJO WAS CREATED
BY MISH & LOOSH

TEXT & DESIGN (INC. MAIN FONT)
2024© MICHELLE GORDON

ILLUSTRATIONS
2024© LUCJA FRATCZAK-KAY

THE AUTHORS ARE NOT MEDICAL PROFESSIONALS, AND AS SUCH THE INFORMATION IN THIS BOOK ARE THEIR OPINION. PLEASE SEEK MEDICAL ADVICE BEFORE DRINKING TEAS SUGGESTED. YOU ARE ENTIRELY RESPONSIBLE FOR YOUR OWN DECISIONS AND ACTIONS TAKEN USING THE INFORMATION IN THIS BOOK. THE AUTHORS AND PUBLISHERS TAKE NO RESPONSIBILITY FOR YOUR ACTIONS OR THE CONSEQUENCES OF THEM. MAKE YOUR MAGIC WISELY.

 # INDEX

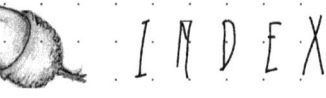 # INDEX

INDEX

 # 2024 BRAIN DUMP

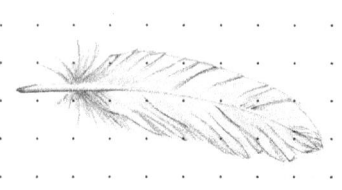
1.0

2024 BOOK LIST

MOON CYCLE DIARY

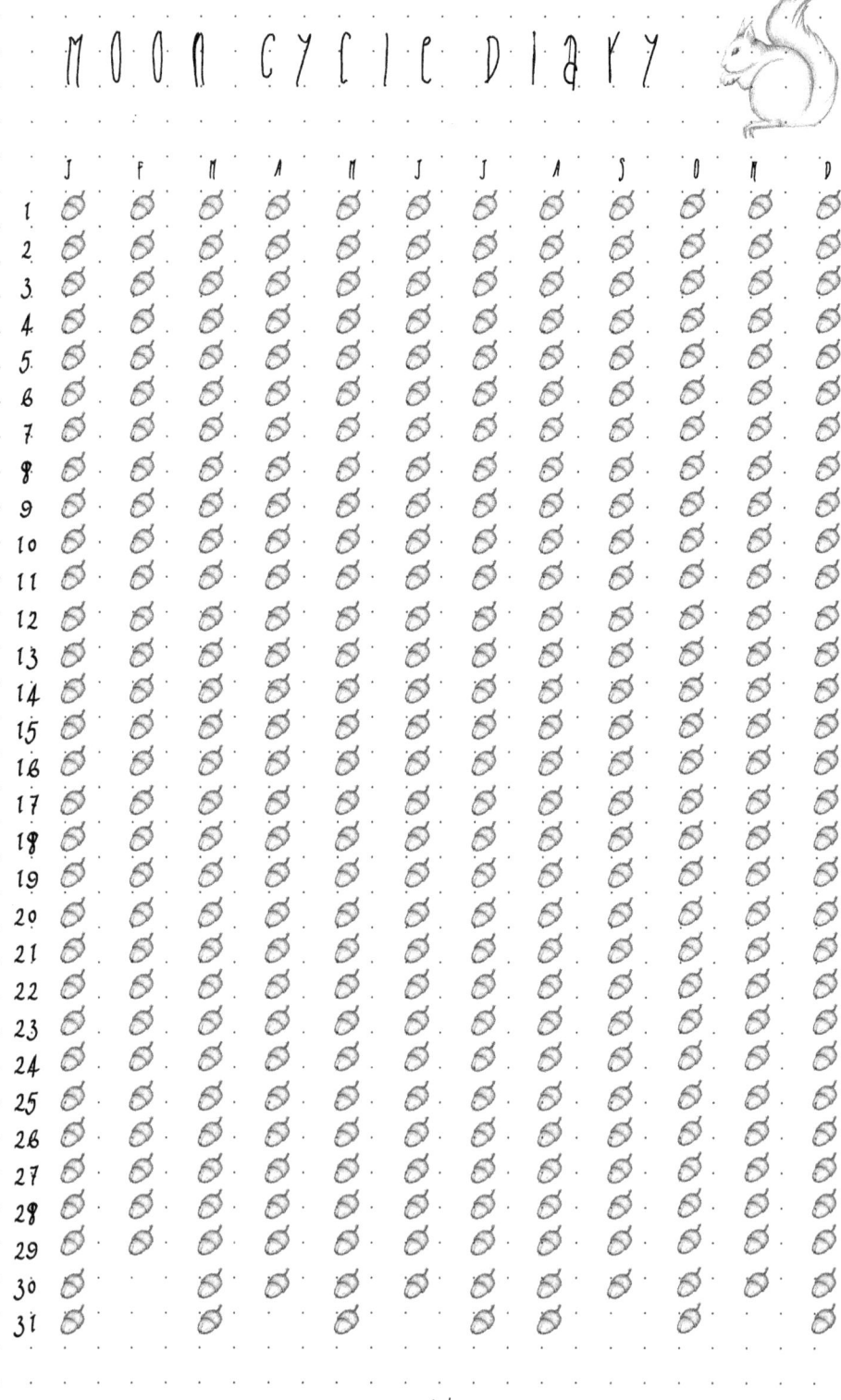

NOTES:

MANIFESTING

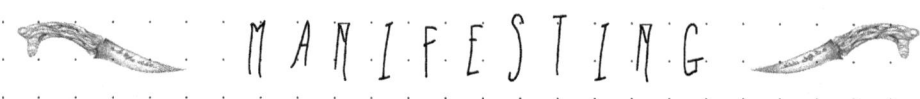

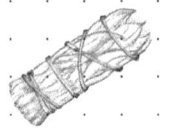 # MANIFESTED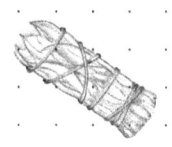

2.2

BIRTHDAYS & ANNIVERSARIES

JANUARY

MAY

SEPTEMBER

FEBRUARY

JUNE

OCTOBER

MARCH

JULY

NOVEMBER

APRIL

AUGUST

DECEMBER

WHEEL OF THE YEAR

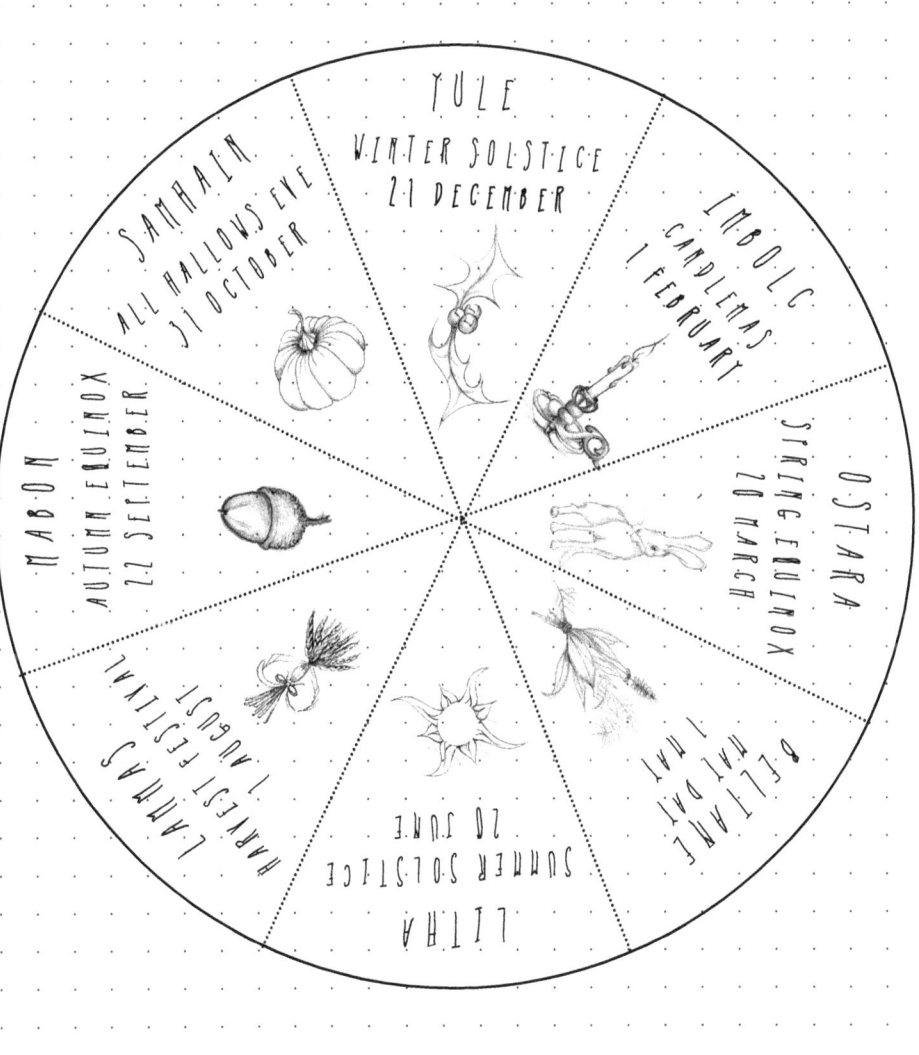

JANUARY

	MON	TUES	WEDS
M 1	1	2	3
T 2			
W 3			
TH 4			
F 5			
S 6			
SU 7	8	9	10
M 8			
T 9			
W 10			
TH 11			
F 12	15	16	17
S 13			
SU 14			
M 15			
T 16			
W 17	22	23	24
TH 18			
F 19			
S 20			
SU 21	29	30	31
M 22			
T 23			
W 24			
TH 25			
F 26			
S 27			
SU 28			
M 29			
T 30			
W 31			

JANUARY

THURS	FRI	SAT	SUN
4	5	6	7
11	12	13	14
18	19	20	21
25	26	27	28

NOTES:

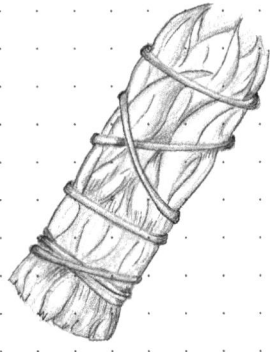

✦ MONTHLY TO-DO LIST ✦

- [ ]
- [ ]
- [ ]
- [ ]
- [ ]
- [ ]
- [ ]
- [ ]
- [ ]
- [ ]
- [ ]
- [ ]
- [ ]
- [ ]
- [ ]
- [ ]
- [ ]
- [ ]
- [ ]

WEEKLY TO-DO LIST

- [ ]
- [ ]
- [ ]
- [ ]
- [ ]
- [ ]
- [ ]
- [ ]
- [ ]
- [ ]
- [ ]
- [ ]
- [ ]
- [ ]
- [ ]
- [ ]
- [ ]
- [ ]

🍄 Weekly To-Do List 🍄

- [ ]
- [ ]
- [ ]
- [ ]
- [ ]
- [ ]
- [ ]
- [ ]
- [ ]
- [ ]
- [ ]
- [ ]
- [ ]
- [ ]
- [ ]
- [ ]
- [ ]
- [ ]
- [ ]

Weekly To-Do List

- [ ]
- [ ]
- [ ]
- [ ]
- [ ]
- [ ]
- [ ]
- [ ]
- [ ]
- [ ]
- [ ]
- [ ]
- [ ]
- [ ]
- [ ]
- [ ]
- [ ]
- [ ]

Weekly To-Do List

- [ ]
- [ ]
- [ ]
- [ ]
- [ ]
- [ ]
- [ ]
- [ ]
- [ ]
- [ ]
- [ ]
- [ ]
- [ ]
- [ ]
- [ ]
- [ ]
- [ ]
- [ ]

HOW TO DOWSE

THERE ARE MANY EXCELLENT BOOKS ON DOWSING, WE RECOMMEND HEAL YOUR HOME BY ADRIAN INCLEDON WEBBER. BUT HERE ARE THE BASICS.
YOU CAN USE RODS OR A PENDULUM, AND THE AIM IS TO GET A YES OR NO ANSWER.

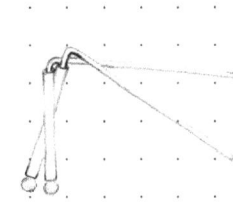

WITH RODS, STAND WITH THE SHORT ENDS LOOSELY HELD IN EACH HAND, WITH THE LONG ENDS PERPENDICULAR TO EACH OTHER. ASK OUT LOUD OR IN YOUR MIND, PLEASE SHOW ME A 'YES', AND THEN SEE WHAT THE RODS DO. THEY MAY OPEN WIDER, OR THEY MAY CROSS OVER ONE ANOTHER. THEN ASK - PLEASE SHOW ME A 'NO' AND MAKE NOTE OF THE ANSWER. YOU CAN NOW ASK YES OR NO QUESTIONS. YOU MAY FIND THAT YOU HAVE A RESPONSE THAT IS MORE LIKE 'MAYBE' OR 'NOT SURE'. TRY RE-WORDING THE QUESTION AND ASK AGAIN.

WITH A PENDULUM, HOLD THE CHAIN BETWEEN YOUR THUMB AND INDEX FINGER, WITH NOT TOO LONG A LENGTH, AND ALLOW IT TO HOVER OVER THE STAR ON THE CHART BELOW. ASK OUT LOUD OR IN YOUR MIND, A QUESTION THAT YOU KNOW THE ANSWER TO, AND SEE IF THE PENDULUM SWINGS TOWARDS THE CORRECT ANSWER. IT MIGHT TAKE A BIT OF PRACTICE, AND YOU MIGHT FIND YOUR PENDULUM SWINGS THE OPPOSITE WAY, THE CHART IS JUST TO GET YOU STARTED, YOU CAN CREATE YOUR OWN CHARTS, WITH MORE ANSWERS AND EVEN COLOURS, EMOTIONS, AND FOOD ETC. TO HELP YOU WITH YOUR ENQUIRIES.

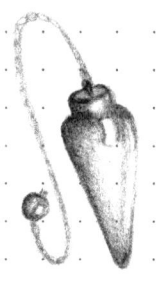

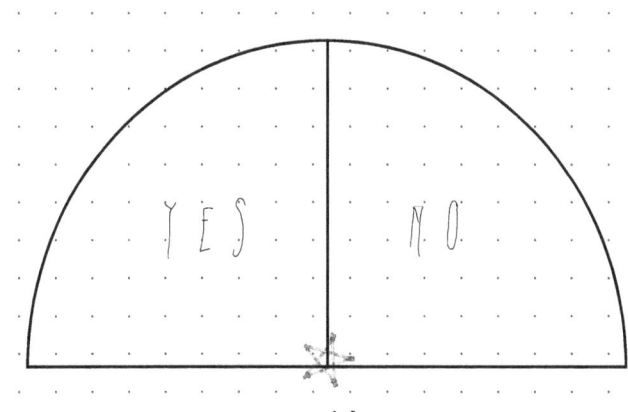

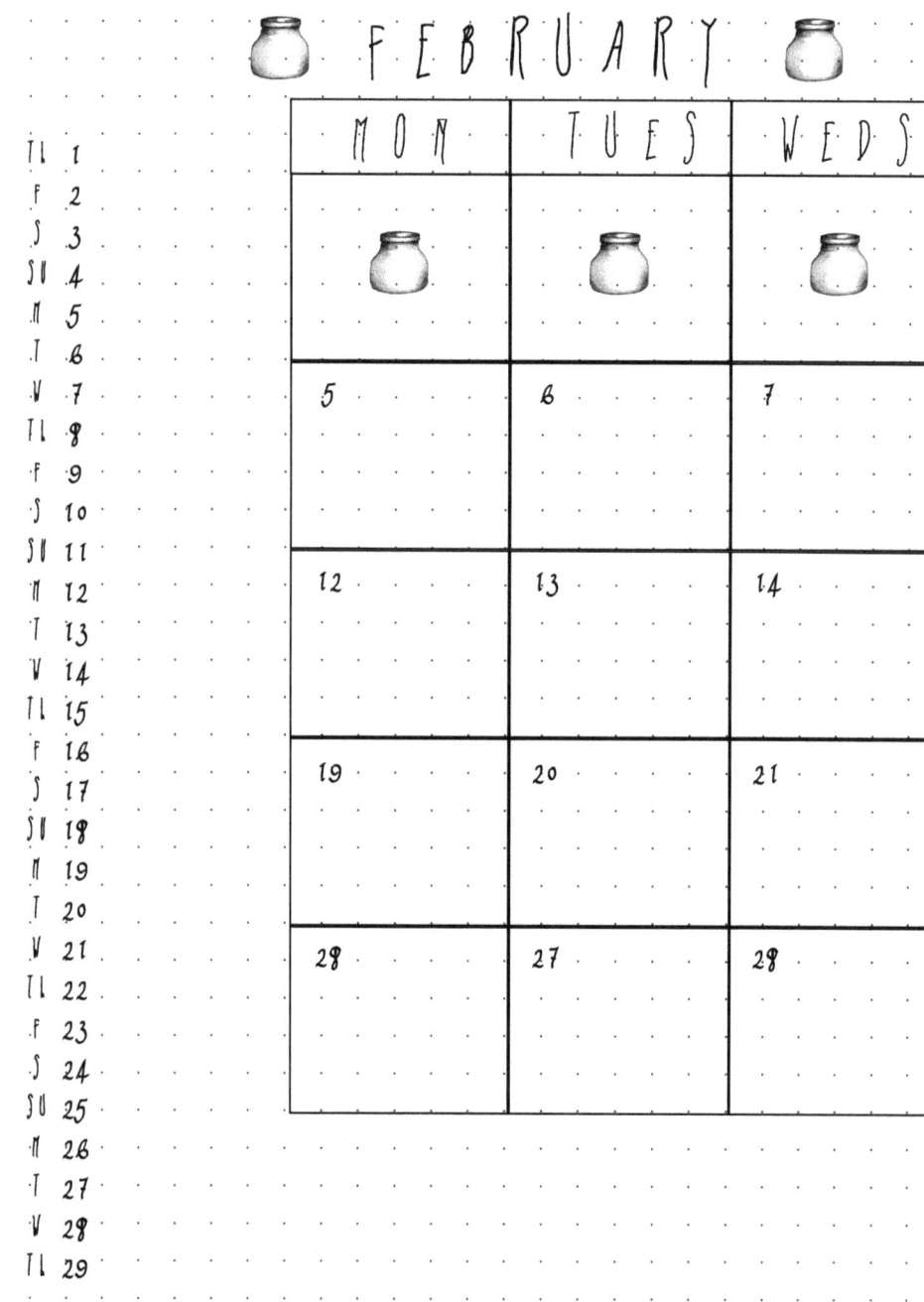

FEBRUARY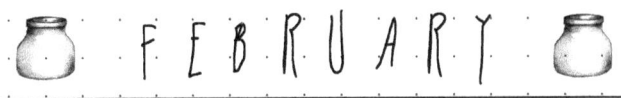

THURS	FRI	SAT	SUN
1 IMBOLC	2	3	4
8	9	10	11
15	16	17	18
22	23	24	25
29			

NOTES:

✦ MONTHLY TO-DO LIST ✦

- [ ]
- [ ]
- [ ]
- [ ]
- [ ]
- [ ]
- [ ]
- [ ]
- [ ]
- [ ]
- [ ]
- [ ]
- [ ]
- [ ]
- [ ]
- [ ]
- [ ]
- [ ]
- [ ]

Weekly To-Do List

- [ ]
- [ ]
- [ ]
- [ ]
- [ ]
- [ ]
- [ ]
- [ ]
- [ ]
- [ ]
- [ ]
- [ ]
- [ ]
- [ ]
- [ ]
- [ ]
- [ ]
- [ ]

WEEKLY TO-DO LIST

- [ ]
- [ ]
- [ ]
- [ ]
- [ ]
- [ ]
- [ ]
- [ ]
- [ ]
- [ ]
- [ ]
- [ ]
- [ ]
- [ ]
- [ ]
- [ ]
- [ ]
- [ ]

🍄 WEEKLY TO-DO LIST 🍄

- [ ]
- [ ]
- [ ]
- [ ]
- [ ]
- [ ]
- [ ]
- [ ]
- [ ]
- [ ]
- [ ]
- [ ]
- [ ]
- [ ]
- [ ]
- [ ]
- [ ]
- [ ]

HOW TO CLEAR YOUR SPACE

Your home, workspace or car can often accumulate energies that may not be beneficial to you, and so it is good practice to clear those energies regularly, so that they don't affect your mood or health. There are many ways to clear your space, you could use the smoke from a smudge stick (we particularly love mugwort smudge sticks, or rosemary), you could burn some frankincense in an incense holder, you could ring a small bell or tuning fork, the vibrations of the sound will clear negative energies, you could use a singing bowl, or if you have no tools to hand, you could also clap your hands to dispel low vibrations, or sing.

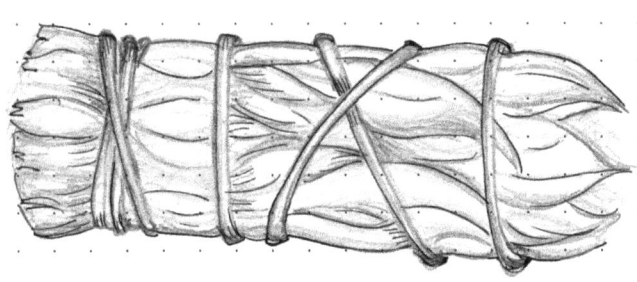

If using a smudge stick, please hold a ceramic plate underneath as you waft the smoke in each room, be careful with any embers that fall off, and extinguish the end of it thoroughly after use.

MARCH

	MON	TUES	WEDS
F 1			
S 2			
SU 3			
M 4			
T 5			
W 6			
TH 7	4	5	6
F 8			
S 9			
SU 10			
M 11			
T 12	11	12	13
W 13			
TH 14			
F 15			
S 16			
SU 17	18	19	20 OSTARA
M 18			
T 19			
W 20			
TH 21	25	26	27
F 22			
S 23			
SU 24			
M 25			
T 26			
W 27			
TH 28			
F 29			
S 30			
SU 31			

NOTES:

MARCH

THURS	FRI	SAT	SUN
	1	2	3
7	8	9	10
14	15	16	17
21	22	23	24
28	29	30	31

MONTHLY TO-DO LIST

- [ ]
- [ ]
- [ ]
- [ ]
- [ ]
- [ ]
- [ ]
- [ ]
- [ ]
- [ ]
- [ ]
- [ ]
- [ ]
- [ ]
- [ ]
- [ ]
- [ ]
- [ ]
- [ ]
- [ ]

WEEKLY TO-DO LIST

- [ ]
- [ ]
- [ ]
- [ ]
- [ ]
- [ ]
- [ ]
- [ ]
- [ ]
- [ ]
- [ ]
- [ ]
- [ ]
- [ ]
- [ ]
- [ ]
- [ ]

WEEKLY TO-DO LIST

Weekly To-Do List

- [ ]
- [ ]
- [ ]
- [ ]
- [ ]
- [ ]
- [ ]
- [ ]
- [ ]
- [ ]
- [ ]
- [ ]
- [ ]
- [ ]
- [ ]
- [ ]
- [ ]
- [ ]

Weekly To-Do List

- [ ]
- [ ]
- [ ]
- [ ]
- [ ]
- [ ]
- [ ]
- [ ]
- [ ]
- [ ]
- [ ]
- [ ]
- [ ]
- [ ]
- [ ]
- [ ]
- [ ]
- [ ]

HOW TO MAKE MOON WATER

DURING A FULL MOON, YOU CAN FILL A JAR WITH WATER, PLACE IT IN THE MOONLIGHT OVER NIGHT, AND IT WILL CHARGE THE WATER WITH A MAGICAL ENERGY. YOU CAN THEN DRINK THIS WATER, WATER YOUR PLANTS WITH IT, OR USE IT TO CLEANSE CRYSTALS THAT ARE WATER-SAFE.

YOU COULD ALSO PUT A LABEL ON THE JAR, WITH YOUR INTENTIONS ON IT.

SUPER MOONS AND BLUE MOONS ARE PARTICULARLY POWERFUL, THE NEXT BLUE MOON WILL OCCUR ON THE 19TH AUGUST 2024.

APRIL

	MON	TUES	WEDS
M 1	1	2	3
T 2			
W 3			
TH 4			
F 5			
S 6			
SU 7	8	9	10
M 8			
T 9			
W 10			
TH 11			
F 12	15	16	17
S 13			
SU 14			
M 15			
T 16	22	23	24
W 17			
TH 18			
F 19			
S 20			
SU 21	29	30	
M 22			
T 23			
W 24			
TH 25			
F 26			
S 27			
SU 28			
M 29			
T 30			

APRIL

THURS	FRI	SAT	SUN
4	5	6	7
11	12	13	14
18	19	20	21
25	26	27	28

NOTES:

WEEKLY TO-DO LIST

- [ ]
- [ ]
- [ ]
- [ ]
- [ ]
- [ ]
- [ ]
- [ ]
- [ ]
- [ ]
- [ ]
- [ ]
- [ ]
- [ ]
- [ ]
- [ ]
- [ ]
- [ ]

WEEKLY TO-DO LIST

- [ ]
- [ ]
- [ ]
- [ ]
- [ ]
- [ ]
- [ ]
- [ ]
- [ ]
- [ ]
- [ ]
- [ ]
- [ ]
- [ ]
- [ ]
- [ ]
- [ ]
- [ ]

WEEKLY TO-DO LIST

- [ ]
- [ ]
- [ ]
- [ ]
- [ ]
- [ ]
- [ ]
- [ ]
- [ ]
- [ ]
- [ ]
- [ ]
- [ ]
- [ ]
- [ ]
- [ ]
- [ ]
- [ ]
- [ ]

6.4

HOW TO MANIFEST YOUR DESIRES

THERE ARE MANY WAYS YOU CAN MANIFEST YOUR DESIRES, BUT WE LIKE TO KEEP THINGS AS SIMPLE AS POSSIBLE, SO OUR THREE FAVOURITE WAYS ARE:

CREATE A SPECIAL BOX TO PLACE YOUR WRITTEN INTENTIONS AND IMAGES OF THINGS YOU WOULD LIKE TO EXPERIENCE, HAVE OR RECEIVE, INSIDE. ADD NEW THINGS TO THE BOX, AND WHEN YOU MANIFEST YOUR DESIRES, YOU CAN GIVE THANKS FOR THE MANIFESTATION, AND THEN BURN THE WORDS OR IMAGES TO RELEASE THEM.

CREATE A VISION BOARD. A SIMPLE PIECE OF CARD COVERED IN IMAGES, WORDS AND CONCEPTS OF WHAT YOU WOULD LIKE TO MANIFEST. YOU CAN TUCK IT AWAY OR PUT IT IN PLAIN SIGHT, BUT KNOW THAT ONCE YOU HAVE PUT THE WORDS AND IMAGES ON THE BOARD, THE UNIVERSE IS ALREADY WORKING ON MAKING THEM HAPPEN.

FINALLY, MISH'S FAVOURITE WAY TO MANIFEST IS TO SIMPLY USE THE SENTENCE OPENER -

I CHOOSE TO TUNE INTO THE REALITY WHERE...

THEN STATE YOUR DESIRE. YOU CAN BE SUPER SPECIFIC, AND YOU CAN JUST SAY IT OUT LOUD IF YOU'RE NOT ABLE TO WRITE IT DOWN. BE WARNED THOUGH, THESE WORDS ARE POWERFUL, USE THEM WISELY!

MAY

	MON	TUES	WEDS
			1 BELTANE
	6	7	8
	13	14	15
	20	21	22
	27	28	29

- W 1
- TU 2
- F 3
- S 4
- SU 5
- M 6
- T 7
- W 8
- TU 9
- F 10
- S 11
- SU 12
- M 13
- T 14
- W 15
- TU 16
- F 17
- S 18
- SU 19
- M 20
- T 21
- W 22
- TH 23
- F 24
- S 25
- SU 26
- M 27
- T 28
- W 29
- TU 30
- F 31

NOTES:

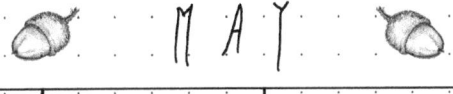

MAY

THURS	FRI	SAT	SUN
2	3	4	5
9	10	11	12
16	17	18	19
23	24	25	26
30	31		

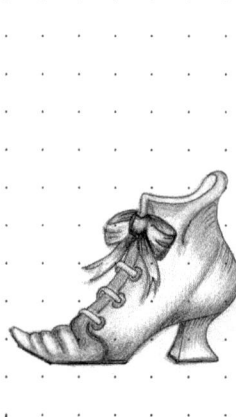

WEEKLY TO-DO LIST

Weekly To-Do List

Weekly To-Do List

- [ ]
- [ ]
- [ ]
- [ ]
- [ ]
- [ ]
- [ ]
- [ ]
- [ ]
- [ ]
- [ ]
- [ ]
- [ ]
- [ ]
- [ ]
- [ ]
- [ ]
- [ ]

WEEKLY TO-DO LIST

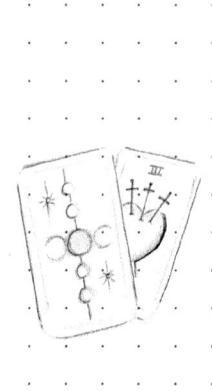

How to Conduct a Simple Oracle Card Reading

Oracle cards can provide help and comfort when we are in need of some guidance, and with such a huge range of cards out there, you can usually get a deck that most resonates with you.

To do a simple reading, simply shuffle the cards, tap them three times to remove any energy of the previous reading, and then fan them out, ask your question silently or out loud, and then select three cards (or the number of cards that most appeals to you). You can either see the three cards as being past, present and future, or just a full answer to your question. Some oracle cards have a full meaning written on the card, some have just an image and one word, you can use the accompanying booklet to get a fuller meaning. If the cards don't answer your question, you can ask again and pull a extra card for clarification.

Keep your cards in a pouch or their box to keep them clean.

S 1
SU 2
M 3
T 4
W 5
TH 6
F 7
S 8
SU 9
M 10
T 11
W 12
TH 13
F 14
S 15
SU 16
M 17
T 18
W 19
TH 20
F 21
S 22
SU 23
M 24
T 25
W 26
TH 27
F 28
S 29
SU 30

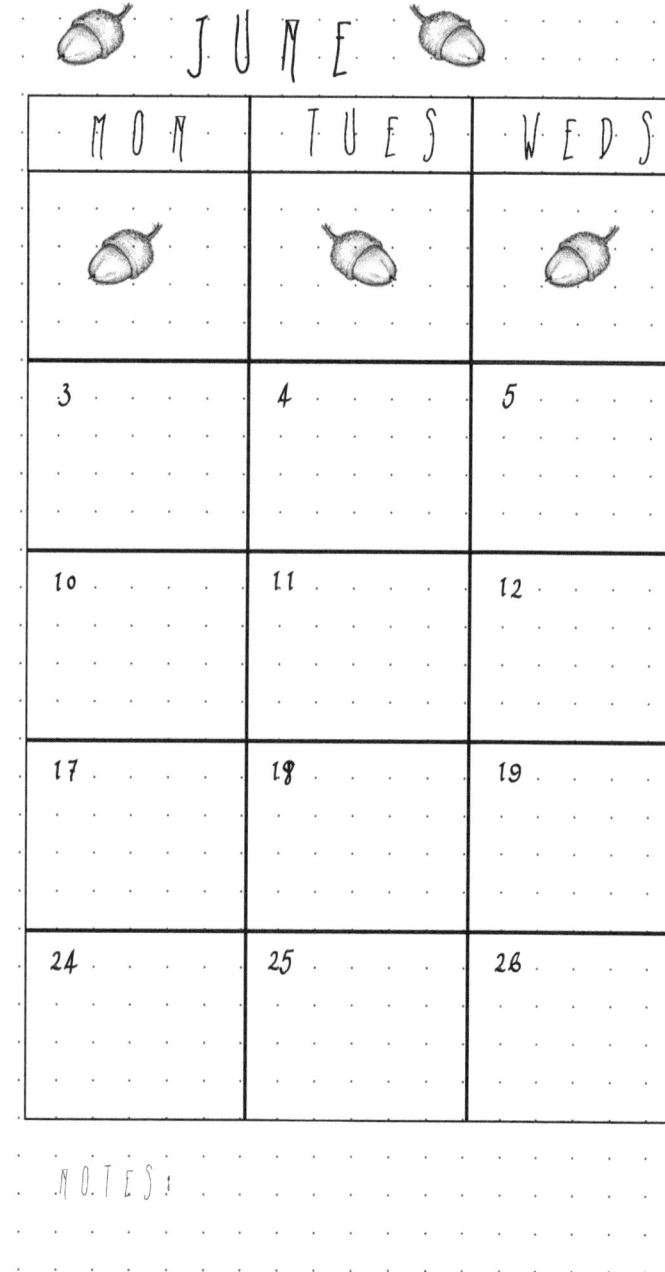

JUNE

THURS	FRI	SAT	SUN
		1	2
6	7	8	9
13	14	15	16
20 LITHA	21	22	23
27	28	29	30

MONTHLY TO-DO LIST

- [ ]
- [ ]
- [ ]
- [ ]
- [ ]
- [ ]
- [ ]
- [ ]
- [ ]
- [ ]
- [ ]
- [ ]
- [ ]
- [ ]
- [ ]
- [ ]
- [ ]
- [ ]
- [ ]

WEEKLY TO-DO LIST

- [ ]
- [ ]
- [ ]
- [ ]
- [ ]
- [ ]
- [ ]
- [ ]
- [ ]
- [ ]
- [ ]
- [ ]
- [ ]
- [ ]
- [ ]
- [ ]
- [ ]

Weekly To-Do List

- [ ]
- [ ]
- [ ]
- [ ]
- [ ]
- [ ]
- [ ]
- [ ]
- [ ]
- [ ]
- [ ]
- [ ]
- [ ]
- [ ]
- [ ]
- [ ]
- [ ]

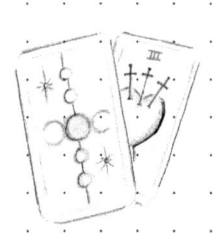

HOW TO CHARGE YOUR CRYSTALS

Sometimes crystals can gather lower energies or become a bit stagnant, to remedy this, you can charge them up again, and cleanse them. Do this regularly with crystals that you wear often.

The best way to charge all crystals is to place them in moonlight or sunlight (be careful with clear spheres, as they can refract sunlight and start a fire!)

Some crystals could be rinsed in water to cleanse, but be wary, as some can dissolve (selenite) and some can give off toxic gasses (raw malachite). It is not a good idea to wash crystal jewellery, as you may damage the metals.

If you have used a crystal for a very intense healing, the crystal may need to be buried for a while, so that the lower energies can be absorbed back into the earth.

Always keep raw and tumbled crystals separate so that they don't damage each other, and keep crystal balls out of direct sunlight.

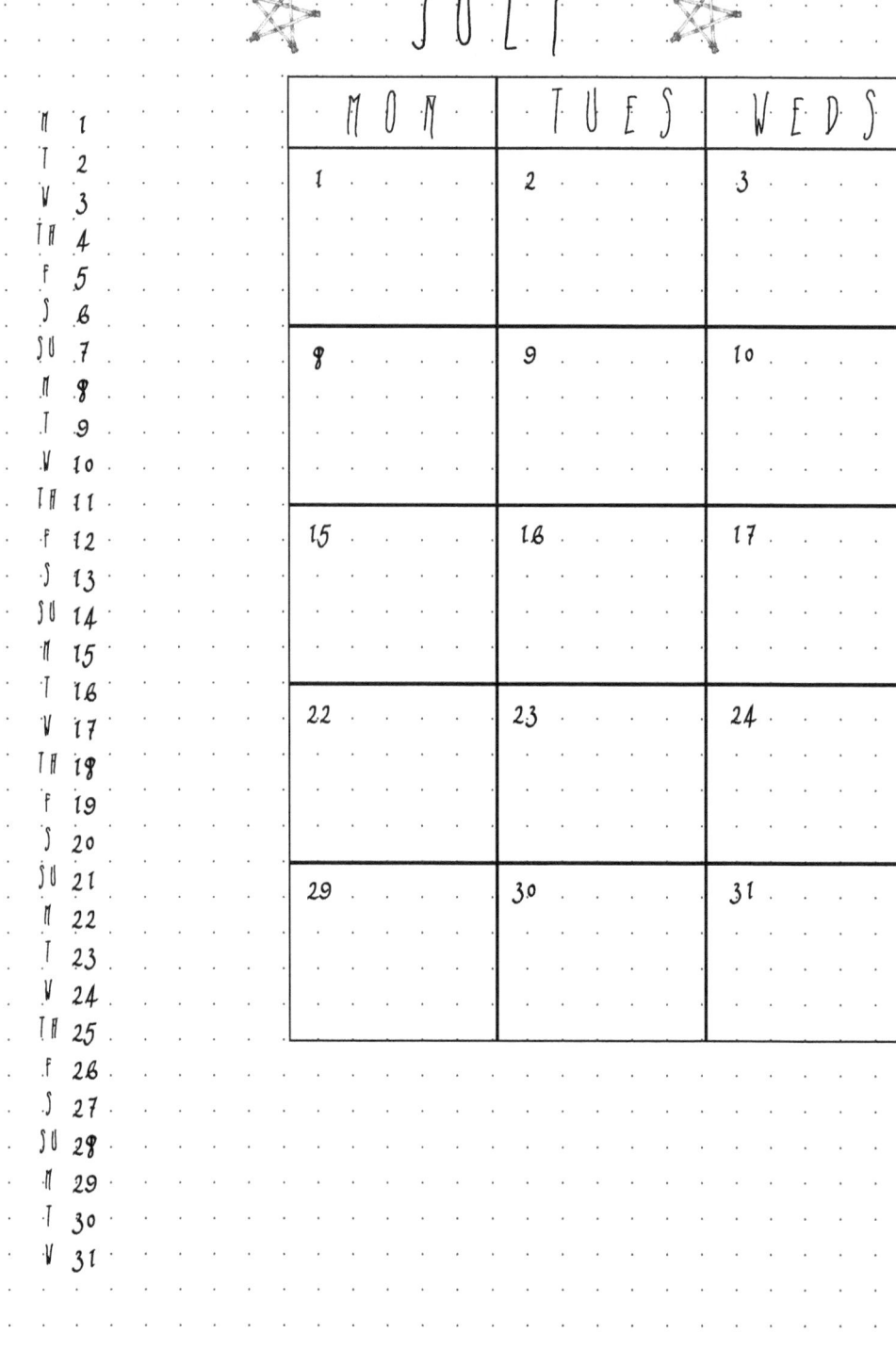

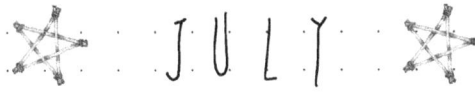

JULY

THURS	FRI	SAT	SUN
4	5	6	7
11	12	13	14
18	19	20	21
25	26	27	28

NOTES:

MONTHLY TO-DO LIST

Weekly To-Do List

- [ ]
- [ ]
- [ ]
- [ ]
- [ ]
- [ ]
- [ ]
- [ ]
- [ ]
- [ ]
- [ ]
- [ ]
- [ ]
- [ ]
- [ ]
- [ ]
- [ ]

WEEKLY TO-DO LIST

Weekly To-Do List

1.4

HOW TO MAKE AN AMULET

YOU CAN MAKE AN AMULET FOR PROTECTION, LUCK, PROSPERITY OR HEALTH. YOU CAN MAKE IT TO WEAR, OR TO TUCK UNDER YOUR PILLOW, OR TO HANG IN THE HOME.

AMULETS SHOULD BE MADE FOR YOUR OWN PERSONAL USE, AND NOT TO TRY TO CHANGE OR INFLUENCE OTHERS. THOUGH PROTECTIVE AMULETS CAN BE USED TO KEEP AWAY ANYONE WITH LOWER ENERGIES OR WHO MEANS YOU HARM.

AN AMULET CAN BE A CORN DOLLY, A SEWN POPPET DOLL, OR A SMALL POUCH CONTAINING HERBS AND CRYSTALS.

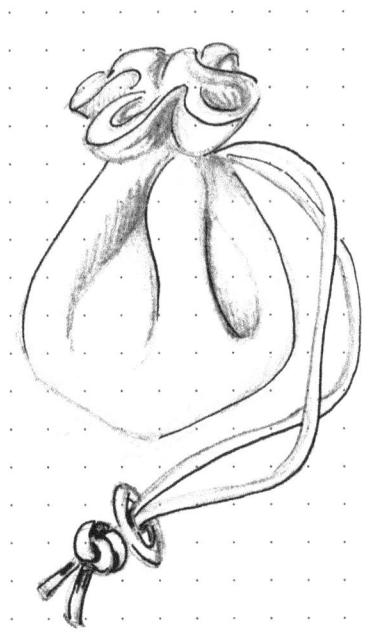

IT IS BEST TO HAVE A CLEAR INTENTION FOR THE AMULET, AND THEN SEEK ITEMS TO COMPLEMENT THAT INTENTION.

FOR EXAMPLE, A PROTECTION AMULET COULD CONTAIN A BLACK CRYSTAL, SUCH AS ONYX OR OBSIDIAN, A FEATHER AND WORDS OF PROTECTION, AND YOU COULD WEAR IT OR PLACE IT NEAR THE DOOR OF YOUR HOME TO PROTECT YOURSELF OR YOUR HOME.

AUGUST

- TH 1
- F 2
- S 3
- SU 4
- M 5
- T 6
- W 7
- TH 8
- F 9
- S 10
- SU 11
- M 12
- T 13
- W 14
- TH 15
- F 16
- S 17
- SU 18
- M 19
- T 20
- W 21
- TH 22
- F 23
- S 24
- SU 25
- M 26
- T 27
- W 28
- TH 29
- F 30
- S 31

MON	TUES	WEDS

5	6	7
12	13	14
19 BLUE MOON	20	21
26	27	28

NOTES:

AUGUST

THURS	FRI	SAT	SUN
1 Lammas	2	3	4
8	9	10	11
15	16	17	18
22	23	24	25
29	30	31	

MONTHLY TO-DO LIST

- [ ]
- [ ]
- [ ]
- [ ]
- [ ]
- [ ]
- [ ]
- [ ]
- [ ]
- [ ]
- [ ]
- [ ]
- [ ]
- [ ]
- [ ]
- [ ]
- [ ]
- [ ]

WEEKLY TO-DO LIST

- [ ]
- [ ]
- [ ]
- [ ]
- [ ]
- [ ]
- [ ]
- [ ]
- [ ]
- [ ]
- [ ]
- [ ]
- [ ]
- [ ]
- [ ]
- [ ]
- [ ]
- [ ]

WEEKLY TO-DO LIST

- [ ]
- [ ]
- [ ]
- [ ]
- [ ]
- [ ]
- [ ]
- [ ]
- [ ]
- [ ]
- [ ]
- [ ]
- [ ]
- [ ]
- [ ]
- [ ]
- [ ]
- [ ]

WEEKLY TO-DO LIST

MOON PHASES & THEIR USES

NEW MOON -
SET INTENTIONS
CREATE NEW GOALS
WORK ON YOUR SHADOW SIDE

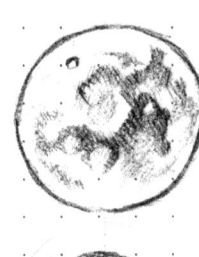

WAXING MOON -
CHECK YOUR INTENTIONS, ARE YOU ON COURSE?
BE CREATIVE

FULL MOON -
CHARGE YOUR CRYSTALS
CREATE MOON WATER
RELEASE OLD BELIEFS & EMOTIONS

WANING MOON -
WRITE A LIST OF THINGS YOU WOULD LIKE TO RELEASE, THEN BURN IT (SAFELY!)

SEPTEMBER

	MON	TUES	WEDS
SU 1			
M 2			
T 3			
W 4			
TH 5			
F 6			
S 7	2	3	4
SU 8			
M 9			
T 10			
W 11			
TH 12	9	10	11
F 13			
S 14			
SU 15			
M 16			
T 17	16	17	18
W 18			
TH 19			
F 20			
S 21	23	24	25
SU 22			
M 23			
T 24			
W 25			
TH 26	30		
F 27			
S 28			
SU 29			
M 30			

SEPTEMBER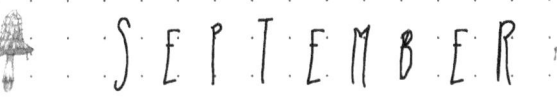

THURS	FRI	SAT	SUN
			1
5	6	7	8
12	13	14	15
19	20	21	22 mabon
26	27	28	29

 NOTES:

✦ MONTHLY TO-DO LIST ✦

WEEKLY TO-DO LIST

- [ ]
- [ ]
- [ ]
- [ ]
- [ ]
- [ ]
- [ ]
- [ ]
- [ ]
- [ ]
- [ ]
- [ ]
- [ ]
- [ ]
- [ ]
- [ ]
- [ ]
- [ ]

Weekly To-Do List

🍄 WEEKLY TO-DO LIST 🍄

- [ ]
- [ ]
- [ ]
- [ ]
- [ ]
- [ ]
- [ ]
- [ ]
- [ ]
- [ ]
- [ ]
- [ ]
- [ ]
- [ ]
- [ ]
- [ ]
- [ ]
- [ ]

Healing Herbs & Their Uses

Rosemary -
Can be burned as a smudge stick to clear your home
Boosts memory

Lavender -
Use in spells for luck
Tuck under pillow to aid sleep

Mint -
Clears the mind, brings clarity, can be drunk as a tea.

Camomile -
Can be drunk as a tea to calm and soothe the soul

Sage -
Can be used in a smudge stick to clear your home
Can be steeped in hot water, then gargled with for a sore throat

Mugwort -
Burn as a smudge stick to clear your space
Write down what you would like to release and burn with some mugwort.
Tuck under your pillow for lucid dreams

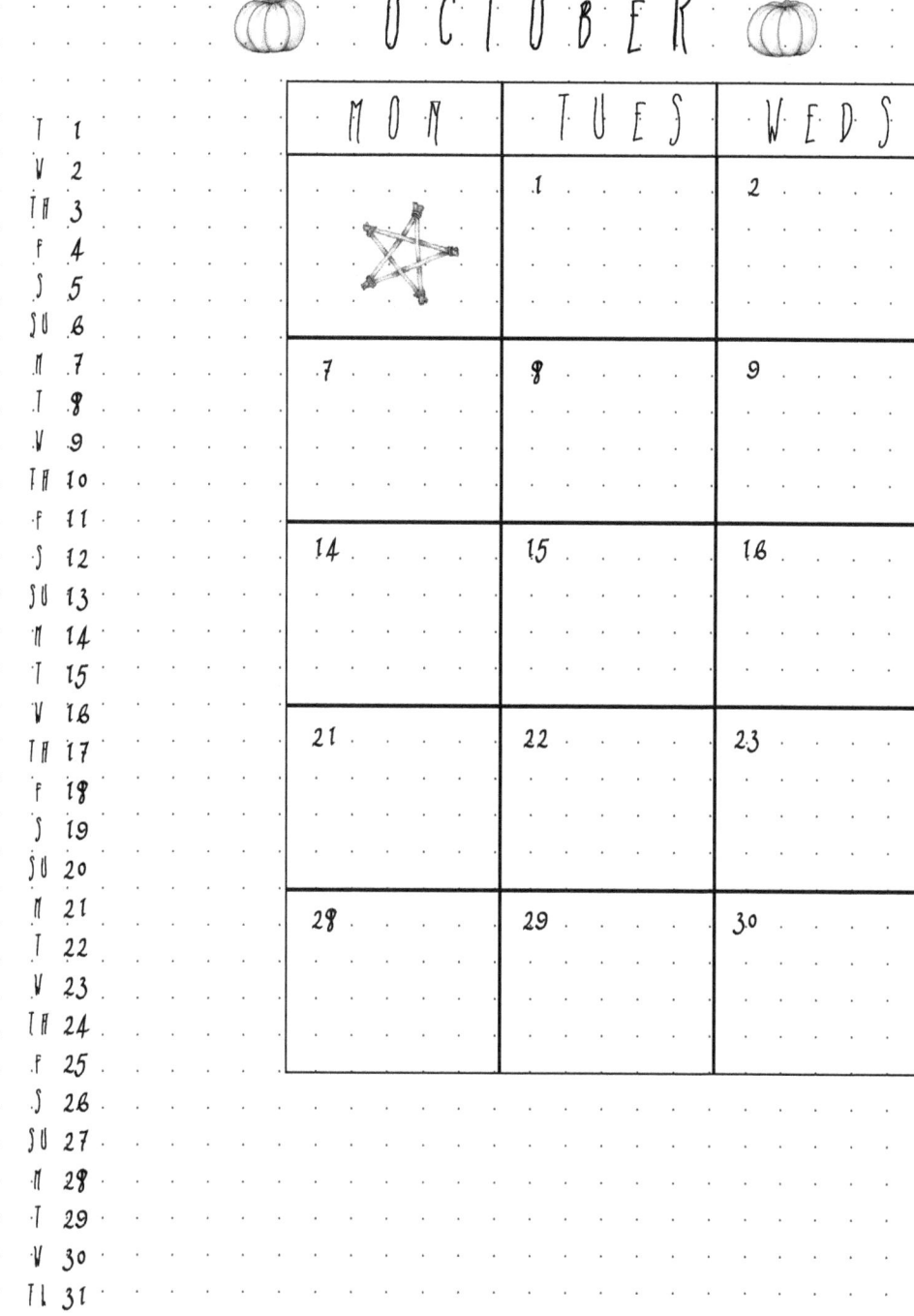

OCTOBER

THURS	FRI	SAT	SUN
3	4	5	6
10	11	12	13
17	18	19	20
24	25	26	27
31 SAMHAIN			

Notes:

✦ MONTHLY TO-DO LIST ✦

WEEKLY TO-DO LIST

- [ ]
- [ ]
- [ ]
- [ ]
- [ ]
- [ ]
- [ ]
- [ ]
- [ ]
- [ ]
- [ ]
- [ ]
- [ ]
- [ ]
- [ ]
- [ ]
- [ ]
- [ ]

WEEKLY TO-DO LIST

- [ ]
- [ ]
- [ ]
- [ ]
- [ ]
- [ ]
- [ ]
- [ ]
- [ ]
- [ ]
- [ ]
- [ ]
- [ ]
- [ ]
- [ ]
- [ ]
- [ ]

Weekly To-Do List

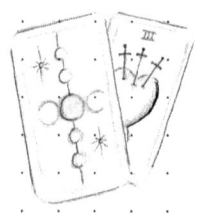

CHAKRAS

CROWN
PURPLE

THIRD EYE
INDIGO

THROAT
LIGHT BLUE

HEART
GREEN

SOLAR PLEXUS
YELLOW

SACRAL
ORANGE

ROOT
RED

When your chakras, which are the seven energy centres of the body, are clear, healthy and spinning freely, your mind, body and spirit will be in balance.

You can dowse to check if your chakras are balanced, and if they are not, you can remedy it by wearing clothing or a crystals of the same colour as the chakra, have reiki, or visualise the chakra that is stuck or unbalanced as bright, and spinning with ease.

To ground yourself, imagine tree roots extending from your root chakra, through your feet and into the earth.

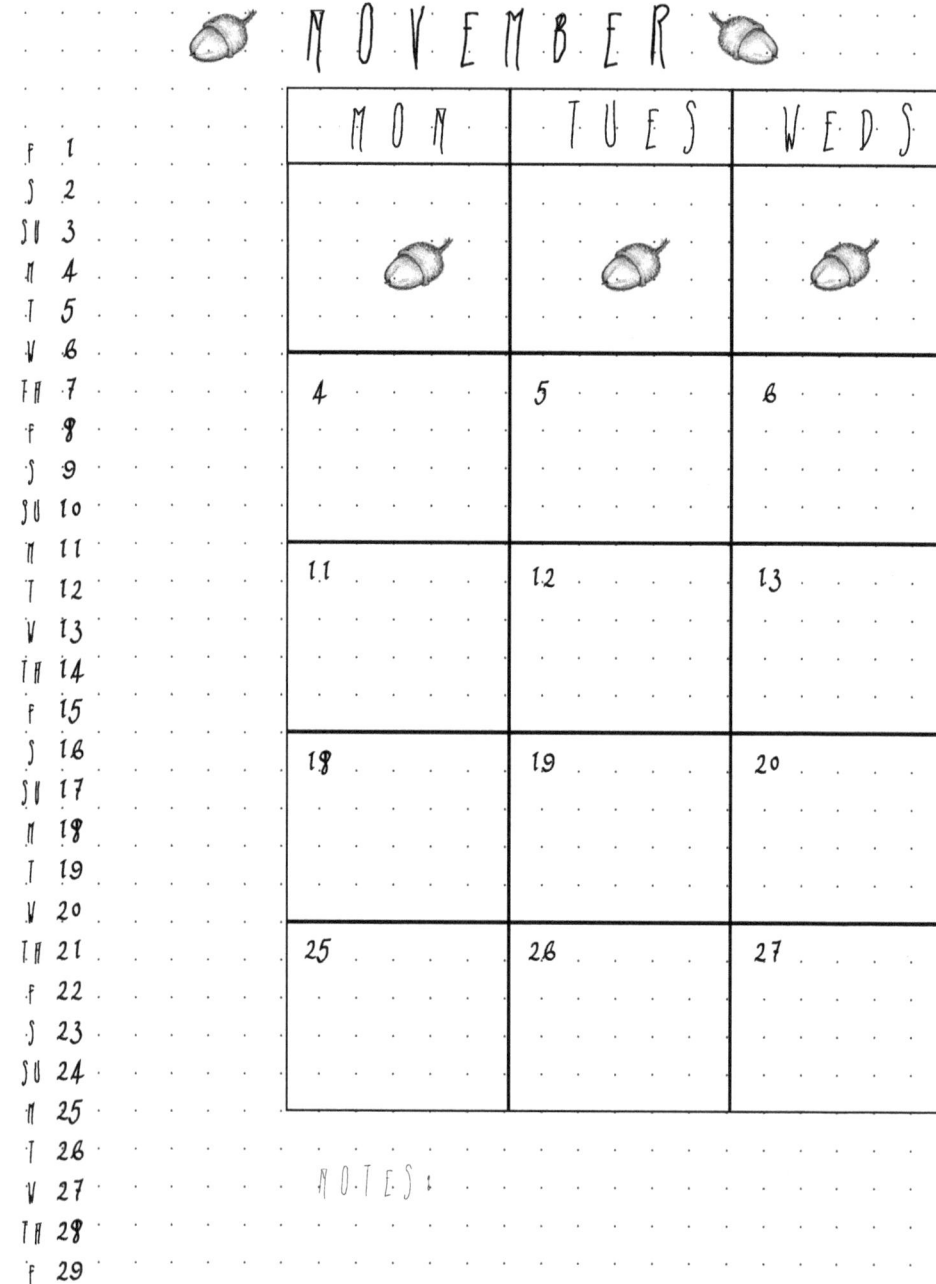

NOVEMBER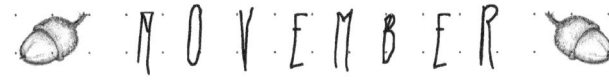

THURS	FRI	SAT	SUN
	1	2	3
7	8	9	10
14	15	16	17
21	22	23	24
28	29	30	

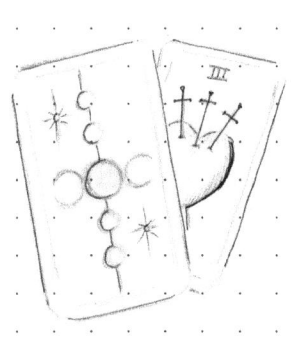

WEEKLY TO-DO LIST

- [ ]
- [ ]
- [ ]
- [ ]
- [ ]
- [ ]
- [ ]
- [ ]
- [ ]
- [ ]
- [ ]
- [ ]
- [ ]
- [ ]
- [ ]
- [ ]
- [ ]
- [ ]

Weekly To-Do List

WEEKLY TO-DO LIST

- [ ]
- [ ]
- [ ]
- [ ]
- [ ]
- [ ]
- [ ]
- [ ]
- [ ]
- [ ]
- [ ]
- [ ]
- [ ]
- [ ]
- [ ]
- [ ]
- [ ]
- [ ]

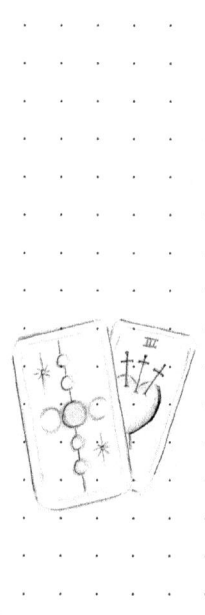

GRATITUDE

Developing an "attitude of gratitude" takes conscious effort, and it certainly doesn't come naturally to most of us, so we would like to share our favourite ways to hone your gratitude skills.

Write a letter to your future self, thanking you for all that you have achieved in the last year. Write it as though everything has already happened, and how grateful you are for it all. Seal the letter and open it in a year's time.

Use the gratitude pages to write down everything that you are grateful for this year, from the tiny things to the big things. What have you done, received, given, enjoyed, loved etc.?

Write thank you letters to friends and family, for gifts or cards they have sent, for their love, their time and their support.

When something good happens, or you receive anything that you want, say out loud - thank you, universe, more please!

Find an organisation that helps those who have little, and donate money goods or your time. By giving to those who have little, without expecting anything in return, you are showing the universe that you have plenty, and thus the universe will bring you more.

Keep a gratitude list or journal through out the year, or fill a jar with little notes of gratitude, then at the end of the year, read through them.

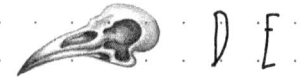 # DECEMBER

	MON	TUES	WEDS
SU 1 M 2 T 3 W 4 TH 5 F 6			
S 7 SU 8 M 9 T 10 W 11	2	3	4
TH 12 F 13 S 14 SU 15 M 16	9	10	11
T 17 W 18 TH 19 F 20 S 21 SU 22	16	17	18
M 23 T 24 W 25 TH 26 F 27 S 28	23	24	25
SU 29 M 30 T 31	30	31	

DECEMBER

THURS	FRI	SAT	SUN
			1
5	6	7	8
12	13	14	15
19	20	21 YULE	22
26	27	28	29

NOTES:

✦ MONTHLY TO-DO LIST ✦

- [ ]
- [ ]
- [ ]
- [ ]
- [ ]
- [ ]
- [ ]
- [ ]
- [ ]
- [ ]
- [ ]
- [ ]
- [ ]
- [ ]
- [ ]
- [ ]
- [ ]
- [ ]
- [ ]

🍄 Weekly To-Do List 🍄

- [ ]
- [ ]
- [ ]
- [ ]
- [ ]
- [ ]
- [ ]
- [ ]
- [ ]
- [ ]
- [ ]
- [ ]
- [ ]
- [ ]
- [ ]
- [ ]
- [ ]
- [ ]

WEEKLY TO-DO LIST

- [ ]
- [ ]
- [ ]
- [ ]
- [ ]
- [ ]
- [ ]
- [ ]
- [ ]
- [ ]
- [ ]
- [ ]
- [ ]
- [ ]
- [ ]
- [ ]
- [ ]
- [ ]

WEEKLY TO-DO LIST

- [ ]
- [ ]
- [ ]
- [ ]
- [ ]
- [ ]
- [ ]
- [ ]
- [ ]
- [ ]
- [ ]
- [ ]
- [ ]
- [ ]
- [ ]
- [ ]
- [ ]
- [ ]

I AM SO GRATEFUL FOR

- [ ]
- [ ]
- [ ]
- [ ]
- [ ]
- [ ]
- [ ]
- [ ]
- [ ]
- [ ]
- [ ]
- [ ]
- [ ]
- [ ]
- [ ]
- [ ]
- [ ]
- [ ]

I AM SO GRATEFUL FOR

- [ ]
- [ ]
- [ ]
- [ ]
- [ ]
- [ ]
- [ ]
- [ ]
- [ ]
- [ ]
- [ ]
- [ ]
- [ ]
- [ ]
- [ ]
- [ ]
- [ ]
- [ ]
- [ ]
- [ ]

ADDRESSES

NAME:
ADDRESS:

EMAIL:
PHONE:

NAME:
ADDRESS:

EMAIL:
PHONE:

NAME:
ADDRESS:

EMAIL:
PHONE:

NAME:
ADDRESS:

EMAIL:
PHONE:

ADDRESSES

NAME:
ADDRESS:

EMAIL:
PHONE:

NAME:
ADDRESS:

EMAIL:
PHONE:

NAME:
ADDRESS:

EMAIL:
PHONE:

NAME:
ADDRESS:

EMAIL:
PHONE:

ADDRESSES

NAME:
ADDRESS:

EMAIL:
PHONE:

NAME:
ADDRESS:

EMAIL:
PHONE:

NAME:
ADDRESS:

EMAIL:
PHONE:

NAME:
ADDRESS:

EMAIL:
PHONE:

ADDRESSES

NAME:
ADDRESS:

EMAIL:
PHONE:

NAME:
ADDRESS:

EMAIL:
PHONE:

NAME:
ADDRESS:

EMAIL:
PHONE:

NAME:
ADDRESS:

EMAIL:
PHONE:

ADDRESSES

NAME:
ADDRESS:

EMAIL:
PHONE:

NAME:
ADDRESS:

EMAIL:
PHONE:

NAME:
ADDRESS:

EMAIL:
PHONE:

NAME:
ADDRESS:

EMAIL:
PHONE:

ADDRESSES

NAME:
ADDRESS:

EMAIL:
PHONE:

NAME:
ADDRESS:

EMAIL:
PHONE:

NAME:
ADDRESS:

EMAIL:
PHONE:

NAME:
ADDRESS:

EMAIL:
PHONE:

ADDRESSES

NAME:
ADDRESS:

EMAIL:
PHONE:

NAME:
ADDRESS:

EMAIL:
PHONE:

NAME:
ADDRESS:

EMAIL:
PHONE:

NAME:
ADDRESS:

EMAIL:
PHONE:

ADDRESSES

NAME:
ADDRESS:

EMAIL:
PHONE:

NAME:
ADDRESS:

EMAIL:
PHONE:

NAME:
ADDRESS:

EMAIL:
PHONE:

NAME:
ADDRESS:

EMAIL:
PHONE:

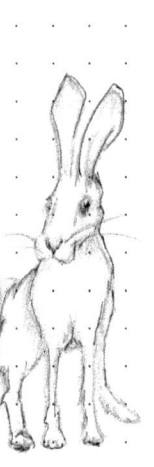

www.ingramcontent.com/pod-product-compliance
Lightning Source LLC
Chambersburg PA
CBHW041304240426
43661CB00011B/1020